CHOCOLATE

QUICK & EASY
CHOCOLATE

70 imaginative recipes
for the busy cook

Gina Steer

Howell Press

HOWELL PRESS
Published in the United States 1994 by
Howell Press, Inc., 1147 River Road,
Suite 2, Charlottesville, VA 22901.
Telephone 804-977-4006

ISBN: 0 943231-74-4

CREDITS

Managing Editor Samantha Gray
Art Director Jane Forster
Photographer Sue Atkinson
Home Economist Gina Steer
Typeset by Bookworm Typesetting, Manchester
Color Separation by Scantrans Pte. Ltd., Singapore
Jacket Border by Susan Williams (Home Economist)
Edward Allwright (Photographer)
Acorn Studios plc, London
(Computer Graphics)
Printed in Belgium by Proost International Book Production

NOTE
The following abbreviations have been used to save space:
tsp = teaspoon
tbsp = tablespoon
oz = ounce
lb = pound

Contents

Introduction

At the word chocolate, eyes light up. Universally popular, chocolate is credited with magical and aphrodisiac powers due to its natural amphetamine, which stimulates the central nervous system and gives a feeling of comfort and well-being.

TYPES OF CHOCOLATE

When you are buying chocolate, it is worth buying the best you can afford. This means comparing labels and looking for the brand with the largest amount of cocoa liquor and cocoa butter. These are the two ingredients that give different chocolates their flavors and characteristics.

These are the types of chocolate you will find on supermarket shelves and at specialist gourmet stores.

Bittersweet Do not confuse this with bitter, or unsweetened chocolate. Bittersweet chocolate is interchangeable with semisweet (see below), but it gives a dish a slightly less sweet flavor.

Semisweet Probably the most popular type of chocolate for home baking, this is a combination of chocolate liquor, cocoa butter and sugar. By law, a chocolate must contain at least 35% chocolate liquor to be labeled semisweet. It is sold in bars, chunks and pieces, or chips.

Unsweetened Also called bitter or baking chocolate, this is pure chocolate liquor, although some brands may contain a small amount of cocoa butter. It is used in baking, but most people find it too bitter to eat on its own.

Unsweetened Cocoa Powder A by-product of chocolate production, cocoa powder is what is left after cocoa butter has been extracted from the cocoa liquor. It is ground to a powder and used to give a deep chocolate flavor to baked goods and desserts.

White chocolate Also called confectioners' chocolate or coating, this is a commercial product that is not a true chocolate because it doesn't contain any chocolate liquor and the cocoa butter has been replaced with vegetable fat.

BASIC TECHNIQUES

To melt chocolate

Take care when melting chocolate for, if overheated, it can burn or scorch, becoming hard and grainy. If this happens, add 1 tsp of white vegetable fat to 3 oz chocolate and stir gently until the chocolate becomes soft and smooth. However, do not add any more than 1 tbsp altogether and do not try to use butter, margarine or vegetable oil.

Melt chocolate in a small heatproof bowl over a pan of simmering water, breaking the chocolate into small squares first. Take care that the bottom of the bowl does not touch the water. Once the chocolate melts, stir gently until it is smooth and free from lumps. If melting the chocolate with a liquid, add this to the chocolate at the start. However, add butter to the chocolate after it melts and before stirring.

To melt chocolate in a microwave, place small squares in a microwave-proof bowl. Heat on High for 1 to 2 minutes, then remove from the microwave and stir until smooth.

Alternatively, place small squares of chocolate in a shallow dish in the oven at 225°F and leave until soft.

To make apricot glaze
(Makes enough to glaze an 8½-inch cake)
Heat 3 tbsp apricot jam and 1 tbsp lemon juice in a pan, stirring occasionally, until almost boiling. Remove from the heat, then rub through a fine metal strainer.

To make vanilla buttercream
(Makes 9 oz buttercream)
Beat 6 tbsp softened butter or margarine in a bowl using a wooden spoon until creamy. Gradually beat in 1½ cups sifted confectioners' sugar, then add 1 tbsp warm water to make a soft consistency. Beat in 1 tsp vanilla extract.

To make chocolate buttercream, omit the water and beat in 2 oz semisweet chocolate.

Baking Techniques

• Weigh or measure your ingredients accurately.

• Either butter or margarine can be used in baking. Both will give excellent results.

• Always preheat the oven before baking. Allow 10 minutes for it to reach a temperature of up to 375°F, and at least 15 minutes for any higher temperature.

• To prevent cakes from sticking to the bottom of cake pans, lightly oil the bottoms and line with nonstick baking parchment or waxed paper so that cakes can be lifted out easily.

• When beating eggs and sugar until thick and creamy, either beat in a large bowl placed over a pan of gently simmering water, ensuring that the bottom of the bowl does not touch the water, or use a food mixer with the balloon whisk attached. Beat the mixture until a trail doesn't immediately sink away when the beaters or whisk are dragged across the surface.

• To test if a cake is baked, insert a clean skewer into the center for a couple of seconds, then remove it. If the skewer comes out clean, the cake is baked. A sponge cake will begin to shrink away slightly from the edge of the pan and the top will be firm to the touch. Test by pressing gently with a clean finger.

• Cool a baked cake in its pan for at least 10 minutes before turning it out. The heavier the cake, the longer it needs to be left to cool in the pan to prevent it from breaking. Never put warm cakes away in an airtight tin; wait until they are completely cold.

Chocolate Meringue Pie

INGREDIENTS

Serves 8

For the pastry
2 cups all-purpose flour
1 tbsp grated orange zest
¼ cup blanched almonds,
very finely ground
2 tbsp light brown sugar
¾ cup margarine
1 egg yolk

For the filling
½ cup cornstarch
4 oz semisweet chocolate,
grated
2 tbsp butter
2 tbsp light brown sugar
2 eggs, beaten

For the meringue
3 egg whites
¾ cup + 2 tbsp sugar

1   Preheat oven to 400°F. Sift the flour into a bowl, then stir in the orange zest, ground almonds, and sugar. Cut in the margarine until the mixture resembles fine bread crumbs.

2   Beat the egg yolk with 2 tsp of chilled water and add to the mixture to bind it into a smooth, pliable dough. Knead the dough lightly, then chill it for 30 minutes. On a lightly floured surface, roll out the dough and use it to line a 9-inch loose-bottomed tart pan. Bake blind for 10 minutes.

3   Blend the cornstarch to a smooth paste with 4 tbsp water. Bring 1½ cups water to a boil, then pour onto the cornstarch, stirring throughout. Pour the mixture into a clean pan and cook over low heat, stirring until the mixture thickens. Remove from the heat and beat in the chocolate, butter, and sugar.

4   Leave to cool slightly, then gradually add the eggs, beating well. Pour the mixture into the pastry shell.

5   Beat the egg whites until they stand in peaks, then gradually beat in the sugar, a little at a time. When all the sugar has been added, pipe or pile the meringue on top of the chocolate filling. Bake for 10 minutes.

6   Reduce oven temperature to 350°F and bake for 30 minutes, or until the meringue is set and lightly golden.

Topsy-Turvy Pudding

1   Preheat oven to 350°F.
Lightly oil an 8-inch cake pan
and line the bottom with waxed paper.

2   To make the topping, heat the sugar and butter in a pan until
the sugar dissolves. Stir, then pour over the bottom of the pan.

3   Drain the pineapple, reserving 2 to 3 tbsp juice, and arrange
the pineapple rings over the topping. Place a whole almond in the
center of each ring, with the remaining almonds in the center.

4   To make the sponge, cream the butter and sugar together in a
bowl until the mixture is light and fluffy, then beat in melted
chocolate. Gradually add the eggs with the ground rice.

5   Fold in the flour with the reserved pineapple juice to make a
soft dropping consistency. Spoon on top of the pineapple, then
bake for 40 to 50 minutes until the top is firm to the touch.

6   Remove from the oven and leave to stand for 5 minutes before
inverting on to a serving plate. Serve hot.

INGREDIENTS

Serves 6

For the topping
6 tbsp light brown sugar

¼ cup butter

8 oz can pineapple rings
in fruit juice

12 blanched almonds

For the sponge
½ cup butter

½ cup light brown sugar

4 oz semisweet chocolate,
melted

2 eggs, beaten

¼ cup ground rice

1 cup self-rising flour

Chocolate Layer Pudding

INGREDIENTS

Serves 4

¼ cup butter or margarine

½ cup light brown sugar

2 eggs, separated

3 oz semisweet chocolate,
melted

½ cup self-rising flour

1¼ cups milk

1 lb plums, halved and
pitted

1 tsp confectioners'
sugar, sifted

1   Preheat oven to 400°F. Lightly oil a 5-cup baking dish.

2   Cream the butter or margarine and sugar together in a bowl until light and fluffy.

3   Add the egg yolks, beat well, then stir in the melted chocolate and flour.

4   Gradually stir in the milk.

5   Beat the egg whites in another bowl until stiff. Fold them into the mixture and mix well together. Reserve one plum half for decoration and then arrange the remaining plums in the bottom of the dish.

6   Pour the chocolate mixture over the plums. Stand the dish in a roasting pan. Fill the pan with sufficient boiling water to come half way up the sides of the dish.

7   Bake for 40 to 45 minutes until firm to the touch.

8   Remove the pudding from the oven and decorate it with the reserved plum half cut into slices. Dust with the confectioners' sugar. Serve with cream or custard sauce.

Apricot Flake

1   Preheat oven to 375°F. Place the apricots, apple juice and 1 tsp of the cinnamon in a pan and simmer gently for 15 minutes or until soft, then pour into a 5-cup baking dish.

2   In a bowl, stir together the bread crumbs, shortening, sugar, and remaining ground cinnamon.

3   Mix 2 oz of the grated chocolate into the bread crumb mixture, then spoon over the apricots.

4   Bake for 30 minutes, or until the top is crisp.

5   Remove from the oven and sprinkle with the remaining chocolate. Serve with custard sauce or cream.

VARIATION
Use rhubarb, apples, plums, or cherries in place of the apricots.

INGREDIENTS

Serves 6

2 cups no-need-to-soak dried apricots

1 ¼ cups apple juice

2 tsp ground cinnamon

2 cups fresh white bread crumbs

¼ cup vegetable shortening

4 tbsp light brown sugar

3 oz semisweet chocolate, grated

Chocolate Baked Alaska

INGREDIENTS

Serves 8

2 eggs

¼ cup sugar

⅓ cup self-rising flour,
sifted

2 ½ tbsp unsweetened
cocoa powder, sifted

8 oz fresh fruit, lightly
rinsed

2 tbsp Cointreau

½ quantity Rich Chocolate
Ice Cream
(see page 36)

3 egg whites

¾ cup + 2 tbsp sugar

1 tbsp slivered almonds

1 Preheat oven to 400°F. Oil an 8-inch tart pan with an indentation in the center. If the pan is not nonstick, you will also need a dusting of flour.

2 Place eggs and sugar in a bowl over a pan of gently steaming water. Beat steadily until thick and creamy and doubled in volume. Remove from the pan and continue beating until cool. Fold in flour and cocoa powder.

3 Spoon batter into the prepared pan and tap the pan lightly on the work surface to level the top and remove any air bubbles. Bake in oven for 10 to 12 minutes until cooked.

4 Take out of the oven and leave for 3 minutes before removing from the pan. Place on a baking sheet and leave to cool.

5 Arrange the prepared fruit in the sponge case and sprinkle with the Cointreau. Place the ice cream on top and place in the freezer while preparing the meringue. Increase oven temperature to 450°F.

6 Beat the egg whites in a bowl until they stand in peaks, then beat in sugar 1 tbsp at a time. When you have added all the sugar, cover the sponge and ice cream completely with the meringue. Sprinkle with the slivered almonds. Bake for 4 to 5 minutes or until the meringue is set and golden brown. Serve immediately.

Steamed Chocolate Sponge

1   Lightly oil and line the bottom of a 5-cup pudding mold or heatproof bowl with a small circle of waxed paper.

2   Cream the butter with the sugar until light and fluffy, then beat in cooled, melted chocolate and milk.

3   Add the egg yolks, one at a time, beating well. Stir in the cocoa powder and bread crumbs.

4   Beat egg whites until stiff and standing in peaks, fold into chocolate mixture. Stir lightly until thoroughly mixed, then spoon into the prepared pudding mold and smooth the top.

5   Cover with waxed paper and foil and place in a steamer over a pan of gently simmering water. Steam steadily for 2 to 2½ hours.

6   Meanwhile, make the sauce. Place the toffees, milk and butter in a small pan and cook gently. Stir frequently until the toffees melt. Keep warm. Unmold the pudding on to a warm serving plate and serve with the sauce.

INGREDIENTS

Serves 6

¾ cup butter

¾ cup light brown sugar

3 oz semisweet chocolate, melted

2 tbsp milk

3 eggs, separated

1 tbsp unsweetened cocoa powder, sifted

3 cups fresh white bread crumbs

For the sauce
8 oz vanilla-flavored toffees

⅔ cup milk

1 tbsp butter

Pear and Chocolate Tart

INGREDIENTS

Serves 8

For the pastry
1½ cups all-purpose flour
1 tbsp unsweetened cocoa
powder
½ cup blanched almonds,
very finely ground
1 tbsp sugar
⅔ cup butter
1 egg yolk, beaten
3 tbsp apricot jam

For the filling
6 tbsp butter
6 tbsp sugar
3 oz semisweet chocolate,
melted
2 eggs
¼ cup blanched almonds,
very finely ground
¾ cup self-rising flour

3 firm pears

1 tbsp lemon juice

1   Preheat oven to 400°F. Sift the flour and cocoa powder into a mixing bowl, then stir in the ground almonds and sugar. Cut in the butter until the mixture resembles fine bread crumbs.

2   Stir in the egg yolk with 1 tsp chilled water and mix to make a pliable, not sticky, dough. Knead the dough until it is smooth, then wrap and chill for 30 minutes.

3   On a lightly floured surface, roll out the pastry and use it to line a 9-inch fluted, loose-bottomed pie pan. Spread jam over the bottom and chill while preparing filling.

4   Beat the butter and sugar together until creamy, then stir in melted chocolate. Add eggs, ground almonds and flour and mix to make a smooth consistency. Spread evenly on top of the jam.

5   Peel the pears and cut them in half, then core and slice the halves vertically, taking care to preserve the pear shape, to within ¼ inch of the bottoms. Brush the pears with a little lemon juice and then place them on top of the chocolate filling.

6   Bake the pie for 10 minutes, then reduce the oven temperature to 350°F and continue to bake for a further 40 minutes, or until filling is cooked. Sprinkle with confectioners' sugar, if you wish.

Baked Chocolate Cheesecake

1   Preheat oven to 350°F.
Sift the flour and ground cinnamon
into a bowl, then cut in the butter until the mixture resembles fine
bread crumbs. Stir in the sugar.

2   Add the egg yolk and 1 to 2 tsp chilled water, then mix together to make a soft, but not sticky, dough. On a lightly floured surface, knead until smooth and free from cracks. Wrap up and chill for at least 30 minutes.

3   On a lightly floured surface, roll out the pastry. Use it to line the bottom and sides of an 8-inch loose-bottomed cake pan. Reserve the trimmings.

4   Beat egg yolks and sugar until pale and creamy, then beat in the cream cheese, melted chocolate, and ground almonds.

5   Beat the egg whites in another bowl until stiff. Fold them into the chocolate mixture. Spoon the batter into the dough-lined pan.

6   Roll out the dough trimmings and cut them into thin strips. Dampen the edges, then lay the strips across the top of the cheesecake, forming a lattice pattern.

7   Bake for 1 to 1½ hours, until the top is firm. Remove from the oven and leave to stand for 10 minutes. Carefully remove from the pan, then sprinkle with the sifted confectioners' sugar. Serve warm.

INGREDIENTS

Serves 8

For the pastry
2 cups all-purpose flour

2 tsp ground cinnamon

⅔ cup butter

1 tbsp light brown sugar

1 egg yolk

For the filling
3 eggs, separated
½ cup light brown sugar

1½ cups cream cheese

3 oz semisweet chocolate,
melted

½ cup blanched almonds,
very finely ground

1 tsp confectioners'
sugar, sifted

Chocolate Crêpes

INGREDIENTS

Serves 8

1 tbsp unsweetened cocoa powder

¾ cup all-purpose flour

1 egg

1¼ cups equal amounts of milk and water

1 tbsp sunflower oil

For the filling
1⅓ cups finely chopped no-need-to-soak dried apricots

⅔ cup orange juice

pared orange zest

1 lb cooking apples, peeled and sliced

¼ cup sugar

1   Sift the cocoa powder and flour into a bowl and make a well in the center. Break the egg into the center and add half the milk and water mixture. Gradually stir in the flour from the sides of the bowl to make a thick batter. Beat to remove any lumps, then stir in the remaining liquid. Leave to stand for 30 minutes.

2   Meanwhile, put apricots, orange juice and zest in a pan and simmer over low heat for 5 minutes, then add the apples and sugar and continue to simmer for 10 minutes. Beat with a wooden spoon until a chunky purée is formed.

3   Heat the oil in a small skillet, then pour off excess and use for frying other crêpes. Stir the batter, then pour 2 to 3 tbsp into the skillet. Tilt the skillet slightly so that the bottom is evenly coated, then cook for 2 to 3 minutes until set.

4   Turn the crêpe over and cook for 2 minutes longer. Repeat until all the batter is used. Keep pancakes warm between sheets of greaseproof paper, either in the oven or over a pan of gently steaming water.

5   Place a crêpe on a warm serving plate and spread with a little of the filling and fold over into a triangle. Serve decorated with lemon balm, if you wish.

Chocolate-Orange Soufflés

1   Preheat oven to 350°F. Lightly butter six ⅔-cup ramekins.

2   Melt the butter or margarine in a pan, then add the flour and cook over low heat for 2 minutes, stirring throughout.

3   Remove from the heat, then stir in the sugar and grated orange zest.

4   Beat in the orange juice gradually, then return to low heat and cook. Stir until the mixture thickens and forms a ball in the center of the pan.

5   Remove from the heat and leave to cool for 5 minutes. Add the egg yolks, one at a time, beating well. Stir in the grated chocolate.

6   Beat the egg whites in a bowl until stiff and standing in peaks. Gradually fold them into the chocolate mixture, using a metal spoon or spatula.

7   Spoon into the prepared ramekins, using a metal spoon or spatula. Bake for 15 to 20 minutes until well risen and just firm. Serve immediately, decorated with a little orange zest.

INGREDIENTS

Makes 6

3 tbsp butter or margarine

¼ cup all-purpose flour

2 tbsp sugar

1 tbsp grated orange zest

⅔ cup orange juice

3 eggs, separated

3 oz semisweet chocolate, grated

1 egg white

orange zest to decorate

Parisienne Delight

INGREDIENTS

Serves 6

3 tbsp butter

½ cup all-purpose flour,
sifted

1 tbsp unsweetened cocoa
powder, sifted

pinch of salt

1 tbsp sugar

2 eggs, beaten

For the filling
⅔ cup whipping cream

2 tbsp chocolate liqueur

6 oz seedless black
grapes, rinsed

1 tsp confectioners'
sugar, sifted

1   Preheat oven to 400°F. Dampen a baking sheet with a little cold water.

2   Place the butter and ⅔ cup water in a pan and bring to a boil. Remove from heat and stir in flour, cocoa powder, salt, and sugar. Beat well until mixture forms a ball in the center of the pan.

3   Gradually beat the eggs into the flour mixture to make a smooth and glossy paste.

4   Place in a decorating bag fitted with a large round tip. Pipe a circle on to the baking sheet about 6 inches in diameter.

5   Bake for 20 minutes, or until well risen and firm.

6   Remove from the oven, make a slit in the side, and return to the oven for 5 minutes to dry out the center. Leave to cool.

7   Whip the cream until thick, then stir in the chocolate liqueur.

8   Cut the ring in half crosswise, and fill the center with the grapes and prepared cream. Sprinkle the top with a little sifted confectioners' sugar.

Chocolate and Brandy Roulade

1   Preheat oven to 350°F. Lightly oil and line a 15 x 10 x 1-inch jelly-roll pan with a single sheet of non-stick baking parchment.

2   Place egg yolks and sugar in a large bowl, then beat until thick and creamy. Beat in melted chocolate and brandy.

3   In another bowl, beat the egg whites until they stand in peaks, then gradually fold them into the chocolate mixture.

4   Pour the batter into the lined jelly-roll pan, tap the pan lightly on work surface to remove any air bubbles and to level the top.

5   Bake for 15 to 20 minutes until a firm crust forms on the top. Remove the roulade from the oven and cover it with a damp sheet of waxed paper and a damp cloth. Leave for at least 6 hours, or, preferably, overnight.

6   Cover a sheet of waxed paper with confectioners' sugar, then turn out the roulade onto the paper. Strip away the lining paper.

7   Whip the cream in a bowl until thick, then spread it over the roulade to within ¼ inch of the edge.

8   Place orange segments over the cream, then roll up as you would a jelly roll. Dredge with a little extra confectioners' sugar.

INGREDIENTS

Cuts into 8 slices

5 eggs, separated

1 cup + 2 tbsp sugar

6 oz semisweet chocolate, melted

4 tbsp brandy

1 tbsp confectioners' sugar, sifted

⅔ cup whipping cream

2 large oranges, peeled and segmented

extra sifted confectioners' sugar

Mandarin Crème Brûlées

INGREDIENTS

Serves 6

2 cups heavy cream

4 oz semisweet chocolate,
broken into pieces

4 egg yolks

¾ cup + 2 tbsp sugar

3 mandarins, peeled,
segmented and soaked in
a little Cointreau

1   Preheat oven to 300°F. Place the cream and chocolate in a large, heavy-bottomed pan or a large bowl standing over a pan of gently simmering water. Heat until almost boiling, stirring occasionally. (Do not allow the mixture to boil.) Stir until the chocolate melts and is smooth.

2   In a bowl, beat egg yolks with ¼ cup of sugar until thick and creamy, then gradually beat in the cream and chocolate mixture. Reserve one mandarin for decoration and divide the remaining mandarins between six ⅔-cup ramekins.

3   Strain the chocolate mixture, then pour it over the mandarins, filling the ramekins to within ½ inch of their tops.

4   Place the dishes in a roasting pan, adding enough boiling water to come half way up the sides of the dishes. Bake for 40 to 45 minutes until the mixture sets. (Do not forget to replenish the water if necessary.) Remove the dishes from the oven, leave to cool, then chill for at least 6 hours, preferably overnight.

5   Preheat the broiler and sprinkle the tops of the ramekins with the remaining sugar, ensuring the custards are completely covered. Broil for 5 minutes, or until the sugar caramelizes. Turn the ramekins as necessary. Chill for at least 30 minutes. Decorate with the reserved mandarin segments and serve.

Marbled Cheesecake

1 Preheat the oven to 300°F.

2 Crush the crackers finely with a rolling pin or in a food processor or blender. Place in a bowl.

3 Melt the butter or margarine in a pan, then stir into the crackers and mix together well. Use to line the bottom and sides of a 7- inch loose-bottomed cake pan. Chill while preparing the filling.

4 Cream together the cheese and sugar until light and fluffy.

5 Beat the eggs with the vanilla extract, then gradually stir into the cheese mixture, beating well.

6 Pour the batter into the cracker-lined pan, add the chocolate and stir lightly with a fork to make a marbled effect.

7 Bake for 30 minutes or until the top feels firm to the touch.

8 Turn off the oven and leave the cheesecake to cool in the oven. Remove from the oven and chill in the refrigerator for at least 6 hours, preferably overnight.

9 Remove from the pan carefully, then decorate.

INGREDIENTS

Serves 8

8 oz chocolate-coated Graham cracker crumbs

½ cup butter or margarine

3 cups lowfat soft cheese

½ cup sugar

2 eggs

1 tsp vanilla extract

3 oz semisweet chocolate, melted

Chocolate Soufflé

INGREDIENTS

Serves 6

4 eggs

2 tbsp sugar

4 oz semisweet chocolate, melted

just under ½ oz unflavored gelatin

1 ¼ cups whipping cream

6 oz white chocolate, grated

1 cup raspberries, rinsed

mint sprig, to decorate

1   Separate the eggs and place the yolks and sugar in a large bowl over a pan of gently simmering water, then beat until thick and creamy. Remove the bowl from the pan and continue beating until the mixture is cool. Beat in the melted chocolate.

2   In a small bowl, dissolve the gelatin in ¼ cup very hot but not boiling water, then fold it into the chocolate mixture.

3   In another bowl, whip the cream until softly peaking, then fold it into the chocolate mixture.

4   In another bowl, beat the egg whites until they are stiff but not dry, then gradually fold them into the soufflé mixture, taking care not to over mix.

5   Place a clean, empty jelly jar in the center of a glass serving bowl, then spoon in a layer of the soufflé batter.

6   Cover the soufflé batter with half the grated white chocolate. Repeat the layers, ending with a layer of soufflé batter.

7   Chill the soufflé for at least 4 hours, or until firm.

8   Fill the jelly jar with almost boiling water, leave for a couple of seconds, then ease out the jar carefully. Fill center with the raspberries and decorate.

Bavarian Cream

1 Beat together the egg yolks and sugar until thick and creamy, then beat in the light cream.

2 Strain the mixture into a heavy-bottomed pan and then cook over low heat, stirring throughout until the custard thickens and coats the back of a spoon. Remove from the heat.

3 Dissolve the gelatin in 2 tbsp very hot, but not boiling, water, and stir it into the custard. Leave to cool. Stir the melted chocolate and sherry into the cooled custard.

4 Whip the whipping cream until softly peaking, reserving 2 to 3 tbsp. Stir the remainder into the mixture, then pour into a rinsed 3¾-cup mold. Leave to set for at least 4 hours in the refrigerator.

5 When set, quickly dip the bottom into very hot water and invert onto a serving plate.

6 Place the reserved cream in a decorating bag fitted with a star tip and use to decorate the sides. Arrange the coconut curls on top of the dessert.

COOK'S TIP
To make coconut curls, crack open a coconut, reserving the milk to use in other dishes or drinks. Remove the shell and then shave off curls from the flesh using a vegetable peeler.

INGREDIENTS

Serves 6

3 egg yolks

¼ cup sugar

1¼ cups light cream

2 tsp unflavored gelatin

4 oz semisweet chocolate, melted

3 tbsp sherry

1¼ cups whipping cream

coconut curls to decorate

Mocha Mousse Tart

INGREDIENTS

Serves 8

1 ¼ cups all-purpose flour

1 tbsp unsweetened cocoa powder

6 tbsp butter

1 tbsp sugar

1 egg yolk, beaten

For the filling
3 oz semisweet chocolate
1 tbsp strong black coffee
1 tbsp light brown sugar
2 tbsp light cream

2 eggs, separated

6 tbsp heavy cream

sifted confectioners' sugar and sugar-coated candies

1   Preheat oven to 400°F.

2   Sift the flour and cocoa powder into a bowl. Cut in the butter.

3   Add the sugar. Add the egg yolk and about 2 tbsp chilled water and mix to a firm but pliable dough. Knead the dough until it is smooth, then wrap up and chill for 30 minutes.

4   On a lightly floured surface, roll out the dough and use it to line a 9-inch loose-bottomed fluted tart pan. Prick the dough lightly, and bake for 15 minutes. Remove from the oven and leave to cool, then chill.

5   Melt the chocolate, coffee, sugar and light cream in a heavy-bottomed pan over low heat. Stir until it is smooth, then remove it from heat and place it in a bowl to cool.

6   Beat in the egg yolks, one at a time. Whip the whipping cream until softly peaking, then fold it into the chocolate mixture.

7   In another bowl, beat the egg whites until they stand in peaks, then gradually fold them into the chocolate mixture. Pour the mixture into the baked tart shell and leave until set.

8   To serve, sprinkle with a little sifted confectioners' sugar and decorate with sugar-coated candies.

Chocolate Marquise Alice

1   Place the egg yolks and sugar in a large bowl over a pan of gently simmering water and beat until thick and creamy. Remove from the heat, and continue beating until cool.

2   Stir the chocolate until smooth, then stir into the egg mixture and mix together lightly.

3   In a bowl, dissolve the gelatin in 3 tbsp very hot, but not boiling, water, then fold it into the chocolate mixture.

4   Whip ⅔ cup of the cream until softly peaking, then stir it into the chocolate mixture with the Tia Maria. Beat the egg whites until stiff and fold them into the chocolate mixture.

5   Pour chocolate into a rinsed 6-inch mold or deep cake pan. Leave to set for at least 6 hours in the refrigerator.

6   To serve, dip the mold or pan very quickly into hot water, then invert onto a serving plate. Whip the remaining cream until thick, then use it to coat the sides, reserving 2 to 3 tbsp for piping around the top. Arrange the cookies closely together around the edge. Decorate the top with whipped cream and chocolate coffee beans.

VARIATION
If preferred, replace the coffee liqueur with cooled coffee.

INGREDIENTS

Serves 6

3 eggs, separated

¼ cup sugar

4 oz milk chocolate, melted

2 tsp unflavored gelatin

1 ¼ cup whipping cream

2 tbsp coffee liqueur

44 chocolate finger cookies or other chocolate cookies

chocolate-coated coffee beans to decorate

Chocolate Pavlova

INGREDIENTS

Serves 8

3 egg whites

¾ cup sugar

1 tsp vanilla extract

1 tsp vinegar

For the filling
6 oz semisweet chocolate

2 tbsp medium-dry sherry

4 oz marshmallows

⅔ cup whipping cream

½ cup slivered almonds,
toasted

1   Preheat oven to 400°F. Line a baking sheet with non-stick baking parchment. Mark a 6-inch-diameter circle in the center.

2   Beat the egg whites until very stiff and dry, then beat in half the sugar, adding 1 tbsp sugar at a time. Fold in remaining sugar. Lightly stir in the vanilla extract and vinegar.

3   Spoon the meringue into the center of the marked circle. Form it into a shell by building the sides up higher than the center with the back of a spoon. Place in the oven and reduce the temperature to 275°F, and bake for 1 hour. Switch off the oven and leave the meringue shell to cool, then place it on a serving plate.

5   To prepare the filling, break the chocolate into small pieces and place in a large bowl over a pan of gently simmering water with the sherry and marshmallows. Heat, stirring continuously, until the mixture melts and is smooth, then remove from the heat and leave to cool.

6   In a bowl, whip the cream until it starts to thicken, then stir it into the cooled chocolate mixture with all but 1 tbsp of the slivered almonds. Cover and chill until required.

7 To serve, pile the filling into the center of the cooled pavlova case and sprinkle with reserved almonds.

Choc-Passion Fruit Charlotte

1   Heat the passion fruit or apple juice until almost boiling, then add 2 tsp gelatin and stir until dissolved. Pour a thin layer into a rinsed 5-cup charlotte mold. Leave to set.

2   Dip thin slices of star fruit and strawberries into the fruit juice and then arrange on top of the set juice. Pour another layer of juice over and leave to set. Dip both the long sides of the ladyfingers into the remaining juice. Arrange them, sugar sides out, side by side around the edge of the mold.

3   Beat the egg yolks and sugar in a bowl over a pan of gently simmering water until the mixture thickens. Beat in warmed milk, before straining into a clean pan. Cook the mixture over low heat, stirring continuously, until thick.

4   Cut the passion fruit in half. Press the seeds through a strainer and stir the juice and melted chocolate into the custard. Dissolve the remaining gelatin in 3 tbsp very hot water and stir into the chocolate and passion fruit mixture.

5   In a bowl, whip the cream until thick, then fold it into the mixture. In another bowl, beat the egg whites until stiff and fold into the mixture. Spoon the mixture into the prepared mold. Leave to set at least 4 hours in the refrigerator.

6   To serve, dip the bottom into hot water, invert and decorate.

INGREDIENTS

Serves 8

1 ¼ cups passion fruit or apple juice

4 tsp unflavored gelatin

½ small star fruit

2 or 3 fresh strawberries

20 ladyfingers

2 eggs, separated

¼ cup sugar

⅔ cup milk

3 passion fruit

3 oz semisweet chocolate, melted

⅔ cup whipping cream

Triple Chocolate Terrine

INGREDIENTS

Serves 10-12

6 oz milk chocolate, grated

¾ cup heavy cream

6 eggs, separated

¾ cup butter

3 tbsp sugar

4 tbsp brandy

6 oz white chocolate, grated

2 tbsp Cointreau

6 oz semisweet chocolate, grated

3 cups raspberries, fresh or frozen and thawed

¼ cup confectioners' sugar

1 Lightly oil and line the bottom of a 9 x 5 x 3-inch loaf pan with nonstick baking parchment.

2 Place the milk chocolate into a bowl and heat 4 tbsp of the cream until just boiling. Pour the cream onto the chocolate, beating until the chocolate melts. Slowly beat in 2 egg yolks.

3 Cut butter into small pieces and beat ¼ cup into the mixture, a little at a time. Stir in 1 tbsp of sugar and 2 tbsp of brandy. Beat 2 egg whites until stiff, then fold into the mousse.

4 Pour the mixture into the lined loaf pan, then place in the freezer until firm. Meanwhile, make the white chocolate mousse. Follow the instructions above, but substitute Cointreau for brandy.

5 Pour the white chocolate onto the firm milk chocolate layer and return to the freezer. Make the semisweet chocolate mousse following the above method and pour onto the firm white chocolate mousse. Place in the freezer until frozen.

6 To make the melba sauce, place the raspberries and sifted confectioners' sugar in a food processor. Blend for 2 minutes, then rub through a strainer to remove seeds.

7 To serve, dip the bottom into hot water for 30 seconds, then invert. Serve with melba sauce.

Crunchy Raspberry Dessert

1   Lightly oil and line the base of a 9 x 5 x 3-inch loaf pan with nonstick baking parchment.

2   Place the hazelnuts, sugar and 2 tbsp water in a heavy-bottomed pan over low heat. Heat gently without stirring until the sugar dissolves. Bring to a boil and boil steadily for about 5 minutes, or until a light caramel forms. Remove from the heat and pour onto a lightly oiled baking sheet. Leave to cool, then grind in a food processor and reserve.

3   In a bowl, whip 1¼ cups cream until thick, then stir in the melted chocolate with the ground caramel.

4   Arrange a layer of ladyfingers in the bottom of the loaf pan, then drizzle 1 tbsp sherry over them. Cover with half the raspberries, then half the chocolate cream.

5   Repeat layers, then finish with a layer of ladyfingers and drizzle over the rest of the sherry. Weigh down and freeze until firm.

6   Carefully remove the frozen dessert from the pan. Whip the remaining cream until thick. Use to cover the top and sides of the dessert. Return to the freezer until required. Leave to soften for 30 minutes in the refrigerator. Serve decorated with lemon balm and macaroons.

INGREDIENTS

Cuts into 10 slices

1 cup hazelnuts, shelled

6 tbsp sugar

2 cups whipping cream

2 oz semisweet chocolate, melted

20 ladyfingers

3 tbsp sherry

8 oz raspberries, cleaned if fresh, thawed if frozen

macaroons and lemon balm to decorate

Chocolate Dacquoise

INGREDIENTS

Cuts into 8 to 10 slices

For the meringue
6 egg whites

2 cups + 2 tbsp sugar

¼ cup shelled and ground hazelnuts

3 oz semisweet chocolate, grated

For the filling
2 cups heavy cream
6 oz semisweet chocolate, grated
3 tbsp brandy

2 fresh mangos, peeled and sliced, or 2 x 14-oz cans mangos, drained

2 cups whipping cream

1   Preheat oven to 275°F and line 4 baking sheets with nonstick baking parchment. Mark four 8-inch circles on each.

2   In a bowl, beat the egg whites until stiff, then fold in the sugar, 1 tbsp at a time, beating well.

3   After adding all the sugar, fold in the ground hazelnuts and chocolate and mix together lightly.

4   Place one-quarter of the mixture into each circle and spread evenly. Bake for 30 minutes, or until firm to the touch. Leave to cool, then remove from baking sheets.

5   Heat the cream, chocolate, and brandy together, stirring until the chocolate melts. Remove from the heat, pour into a bowl and chill for at least 45 minutes. Beat until thickened.

6   Spread one meringue circle with one-third of the chocolate filling. Top with one-third of the mangos. Repeat the layers, ending with a meringue circle.

7   Whip the whipping cream until thick, then use to cover the sides and top. Freeze for 6 hours or until solid. Leave to soften for 30 minutes in the refrigerator before serving.

Chocolate Cassata

1   Soak the golden raisins and prunes in the brandy or rum for at least an hour. Set freezer to rapid freeze. Spoon the vanilla ice cream into an ice cream bombe mold or 5-cup freezerproof bowl and cover the bottom and sides to a thickness of 1 inch. Place in freezer until firm and beginning to freeze.

2   Drain the golden raisins and prunes, then stir them into the unfrozen chocolate ice cream. Rinse the angelica and cherries. Chop them finely, then stir them into the chocolate ice cream and mix together. Place in freezer until vanilla ice cream is firm.

3   Spoon the chocolate ice cream into the center of the mold or bowl, smooth the top and freeze for 6 hours or until frozen.

4   Break the chocolate into pieces. Place in a small bowl over a pan of gently simmering water. Add the butter and milk and heat, stirring occasionally, until the chocolate and butter melt. Stir until you have a smooth sauce.

5   Turn out the frozen dessert and serve with chocolate sauce.

COOK'S TIP
After draining the raisins and apricots, use the brandy or rum in another dessert, such as a trifle.

INGREDIENTS

Serves 8

⅔ cup golden raisins

⅔ cup no-need-to-soak dried prunes, finely chopped

4 tbsp brandy or rum

2½ cups vanilla ice cream, partially frozen

unfrozen ½ quantity of Rich Chocolate Ice Cream (see page 36)

2 oz angelica

⅓ cup candied cherries

For the sauce
6 oz semisweet chocolate
2 tbsp butter
4 tbsp milk

Pear Bombes

INGREDIENTS

Serves 4

4 firm pears

juice of 1 lemon

½ cup + 1 tbsp sugar

6 tbsp mascarpone cheese

1 tbsp chocolate pieces

grated zest of 1 small
orange

6 oz semisweet chocolate,
melted

julienne strips of orange
zest and mint sprigs to
decorate

1   Peel the pears, leaving stems intact. Using a vegetable peeler or teaspoon, remove the core from flower end as neatly as possible. Hollow out the center slightly and brush the pears with lemon juice to preserve their color.

2   In a pan, dissolve ½ cup of sugar in 1¼ cups water. Bring to a boil and boil for 5 minutes to make a light syrup.

3   Place the pears in the sugar syrup and poach gently for 10 minutes, turning frequently until the pears are just tender. Remove with a slotted spoon and drain well.

4   In a bowl, beat the mascarpone cheese with the remaining 1 tbsp sugar, then fold in the chocolate pieces and orange zest.

5   Fill the insides of the poached pears with the cheese mixture and freeze for about 1 hour, or until firm.

6   Remove from the freezer and carefully coat in the melted chocolate. Return to the freezer for at least 30 minutes. Leave to soften in the refrigerator for 20 minutes. Decorate with mint sprigs and serve on a bed of orange zest.

COOK'S TIP
Add a little brandy, rum or coffee liqueur to the cheese mixture and to the sugar syrup for poaching the pears.

Chocolate-Red Currant Sorbet

1   Set the freezer to rapid freeze 30 minutes before making the sorbet. (Don't forget to return the freezer to its normal setting after freezing the sorbet.)

2   Place the red currants, sugar and 2½ cups water in a heavy-bottomed pan, then heat gently until the sugar dissolves.

3   Add the chocolate and stir occasionally until it melts. Bring to a boil and boil for 2 minutes.

4   Remove from the heat and stir in the lemon juice. Pass through a fine strainer to remove the red currant seeds and cool.

5   In another bowl, beat the egg white until stiff, then fold it into the red-currant mixture and pour into a freezerproof container.

6   Freeze for about 1½ hours, then remove from freezer and blend the partially frozen mixture in a food processor. Return to the freezer for a further hour.

7   Repeat the freezing and blending at least twice more, then leave in the freezer until solid.

8   Leave to soften in the refrigerator for 30 minutes before spooning into individual dishes and decorating with red currants and mint.

INGREDIENTS

Serves 8

½ lb red currants, cleaned, stems removed

½ cup sugar

4 oz semisweet chocolate, grated

juice of 1 lemon

1 egg white (optional)

fresh or frozen red currants and mint sprigs to decorate

Rich Chocolate Ice Cream

INGREDIENTS

Serves 8

2 eggs

¼ cup sugar

1 ¼ cups milk

8 oz semisweet chocolate, grated

2 ½ cups heavy cream

chocolate cups, wafers, and strawberry halves dipped into melted chocolate to serve

1   Set freezer to rapid freeze. Beat the eggs and sugar together until thick.

2   Gently heat the milk and chocolate in a pan, stirring until the chocolate melts. Pour the chocolate milk onto the eggs and sugar, then mix together well.

3   Strain mixture into a clean pan, then cook over low heat until the custard thickens and coats the back of a spoon. Remove from the heat and leave to cool.

4   Whip the cream until softly peaking and fold into the cooled chocolate custard.

5   Pour into a freezerproof container and freeze for at least 4 hours, or until firm. (Remember to return freezer to normal setting afterwards.)

6   Allow to soften in the refrigerator for 30 minutes before serving in chocolate cups with the wafers and strawberries.

VARIATION
Try adding 4 tbsp of rum or brandy and ¾ cup raisins to the cooled custard before freezing.

Chocolate-Chestnut Mousse

1   Heat the sugar and ⅔ cup water in a heavy-bottomed pan, stirring until the sugar dissolves. Bring to a boil and boil for 5 minutes. Remove from the heat, then stir in the chocolate and the chestnut purée. Stir the mixture until it is smooth.

2   Place the egg yolks in a large bowl over a pan of gently simmering water and beat until thick and creamy.

3   Gradually beat in the chocolate syrup and then the Marsala wine or sherry.

4   Pour the mixture into freezerproof glasses and freeze for at least 4 hours.

5   Decorate with marrons glacés and orange zest to serve.

COOK'S TIP
If preferred, substitute 1¼ cups heavy cream for the egg yolks. Whip until thick, then beat in the cooled chocolate syrup.

INGREDIENTS

Serves 4

½ cup sugar

4 oz semisweet chocolate

3 tbsp unsweetened chestnut purée

4 egg yolks

1 tbsp Marsala wine or sweet sherry

marrons glacés and julienne strips of orange zest to decorate

Devil's Food Cake

INGREDIENTS

Cuts into 8-10 slices

4 oz semisweet chocolate
¾ cup + 2 tbsp buttermilk
¾ cup + 2 tbsp light
brown sugar

½ cup butter
4 eggs, beaten

2 cups self-rising flour
1 tbsp unsweetened cocoa
powder, sifted

For the frosting
8 oz semisweet chocolate
6 tbsp unsalted butter
1 tbsp light corn syrup

1½ tbsp apricot glaze (see
page 8)

chocolate curls

1   Preheat oven to 350°F. Lightly oil and line the base of two 7-inch round cake pans.

2   In a pan, melt the chocolate with the buttermilk and ¼ cup of the sugar. Stir until smooth, then leave to cool.

3   In a bowl, cream the butter with the remaining sugar until light and fluffy. Beat in the eggs gradually, with 1 tbsp flour after each addition.

4   Stir in the cooled chocolate and buttermilk mixture, then stir in the remaining flour and cocoa powder.

5   Pour the batter into the prepared tins and bake in the oven for 25 minutes or until a skewer inserted in the center comes out clean. Remove from oven and allow to cool on a cooling rack.

6   Make the frosting by melting the chocolate, butter and syrup in a heavy-bottomed pan, stirring until smooth. Remove the mixture from heat and leave until it begins to thicken.

7   Sandwich the 2 cakes together with a little of the frosting. Place the cake on a wire cooling rack and brush with warm apricot glaze. Pour the remaining frosting over the top, smoothing it around the sides with a spatula. Decorate with chocolate curls.

Chocolate Layer Gateau

1   Preheat oven to 375°F. Lightly oil and line the bottoms of two 7-inch round cake pans.

2   Cream the butter and sugar together until light and fluffy. Add the eggs, one at a time, with 1 tbsp of the flour after each addition.

3   Beat in the vanilla extract and grated white chocolate, then add the remaining flour with 1 to 2 tbsp cooled, boiled water to make a soft, dropping consistency. Mix lightly.

4   Spoon into the prepared pans and bake for 20 to 25 minutes, or until a skewer inserted in the center comes out clean. Remove from the oven and cool. Cut each cake in half.

5   To make the filling, cream the butter, chestnut purée, confectioners' sugar and cocoa powder together until light and fluffy.

6   To make the icing, place the chocolate, butter and corn syrup in a heavy-bottomed pan and heat gently, stirring frequently until the chocolate melts and is smooth. Remove from the heat and beat occasionally until the icing begins to thicken (about 15 minutes).

7   Sandwich the cake layers together with half the filling and chocolate icing. Coat the sides with filling, then roll in the chocolate jimmies. Pipe rosettes around the edge of the gateau. Spread remaining icing over the top and decorate with mini eggs.

INGREDIENTS

Cuts into 12 slices

¾ cup butter
¾ cup + 2 tbsp sugar
3 eggs
1½ cups self-rising flour
1 tsp vanilla extract
2 oz white chocolate,
grated

For the filling
¼ cup butter
3 tbsp unsweetened
chestnut purée
1½ cups confectioners'
sugar
1 tbsp unsweetened cocoa
powder

For the icing
6 oz semisweet chocolate
¼ cup butter
2 tsp light corn syrup
2 oz chocolate jimmies
and mini eggs to decorate

Chocolate-Hazelnut Gateau

INGREDIENTS

Cuts into 12 slices

3 egg whites

1½ cups confectioners' sugar, sifted

½ cup hazelnuts, shelled, skinned and finely ground

For the icing
1 cup butter

2 cups confectioners' sugar

8 oz semisweet chocolate, melted

1 tbsp strong, cooled black coffee

3 tbsp rum or brandy

chocolate curls and confectioners' sugar to decorate

1   Preheat oven to 275°F. Line 3 baking sheets with nonstick baking parchment and mark a 7-inch circle in the center of each.

2   Beat the egg whites until they stand in peaks, then gradually beat in confectioners' sugar, 1 tbsp at a time, bringing the mixture back to its original stiffness.

3   Fold in the finely ground hazelnuts. Divide the mixture between the 3 circles. Bake for 50 to 60 minutes until firm to the touch, then leave to cool on a wire rack.

4   Cream together the butter and sifted confectioners' sugar until soft, then beat in the cooled chocolate. Add the coffee and rum or brandy, then beat together well. Leave in the refrigerator until beginning to harden.

5   Sandwich the meringues together using about 1½ tbsp icing on each layer. Cover top and sides with the remaining icing, then decorate with chocolate curls and a little confectioners' sugar.

COOK'S TIP
To make chocolate curls quickly, pull a vegetable peeler or cheese grater over a block of chocolate that is at room temperature.

Chocolate Marbled Torte

1   Preheat oven to 350°F. Lightly oil and line the bottom of an 8½-inch springform cake pan.

2   Cream together the butter and sugar until light and fluffy. Gradually add the eggs to the mixture with 1 tbsp flour after each addition. Fold in the remaining flour and ground almonds.

3   Place half the batter in another bowl and stir in the melted chocolate with 1 tbsp cooled, boiled water. Mix to a smooth dropping consistency. Into the other half, stir in vanilla extract and 1 tbsp cooled, boiled water.

4   Place alternate spoonfuls into the prepared pan and, with a fork, lightly ripple the 2 batters together. Bake for 1 hour, or until the top springs back when touched lightly with the finger. Remove from the oven and leave to cool on a wire rack, then discard the lining paper.

5   Beat the cooled coffee into the prepared buttercream. Reserve about 2 tbsp of the buttercream to coat sides of cake. Roll cake in toasted slivered almonds.

6   Brush the top with warm apricot glaze and sprinkle with the cocoa powder. Use the reserved buttercream to pipe rosettes around the edge.

INGREDIENTS

Cuts into 12 slices

1 cup butter
1 cup + 2 tbsp sugar

4 eggs, beaten

1½ cups self-rising flour

½ cup blanched almonds,
very finely ground

4 oz semisweet chocolate,
melted

1 tsp vanilla extract

1 tbsp strong black coffee
½ cup unflavored
buttercream (page 8)

½ cup slivered almonds

1 tbsp apricot glaze
(page 8)
1 tbsp unsweetened cocoa
powder

Checkered Cake

INGREDIENTS

Cuts into 12 slices

1 cup butter

1 cup sugar

5 eggs

2 cups self-rising flour

⅓ cup blanched almonds,
very finely ground

1 tsp vanilla extract

3 oz semisweet chocolate,
melted

4 tbsp raspberry preserve,
warmed and strained

For the topping
1¼ cups cream
10 oz semisweet
chocolate, grated

1   Preheat oven to 350°F. Lightly oil three 7-inch round cake pans and line the bottoms with nonstick parchment paper.

2   Cream together the butter and sugar until light and fluffy. Add eggs one at a time, with 1 tbsp flour after each addition. Fold in the remaining flour, then the ground almonds.

3   Divide the mixture in half, then stir the vanilla extract into one half and the melted chocolate into the other. Spoon into 2 decorating bags and pipe alternate rings of mixture into the cake pans, reversing the order of piping in one tin.

4   Bake for 20 to 25 minutes, or until cooked. Remove from the oven and leave to cool on a wire rack. Unmold each cake.

5   Sandwich all 3 cakes together with the preserve, placing the cake where piping is reversed in the middle.

6   In a pan, heat the cream to just below boiling point, then pour it over 8 oz of the grated chocolate and stir until the chocolate melts. Cool, then beat until thick and fluffy. Spread the sides of the cake with two-thirds of the icing, then roll in the remaining grated chocolate. Use the remainder of the icing to spread over the top of the cake and to pipe rosettes around the outside edge.

Caramel Torte

1   Preheat oven to 350°F.
Lightly oil and line the bottoms
of two 7-inch round baking pans and
dust with flour.

2   Place the eggs and sugar in a bowl over a pan of gently simmering water and beat until thick. Remove from the heat, then
continue beating until cool. Fold in the sifted flour and cocoa
powder. Add the cooled, melted butter and gently mix together.
Divide between the 2 pans, then bake for 20 to 25 minutes until
cooked. Leave to cool.

3   Mark an 8-inch circle on a sheet of nonstick baking parchment. Place the sugar in a heavy-bottomed pan and heat gently
until dissolved. Do not stir. Bring to a boil, then boil until a rich
caramel color forms. Pour onto the marked circle. When almost
set, mark 10 to 12 triangles and trim the edge.

4   Split the 2 cakes in half. Spread each layer with about 2 tbsp
of the chocolate butter cream. Sandwich both layers together.

5   Spread sides with about 3 tbsp buttercream and roll in the
nuts. Use remaining buttercream to cover the top of the cake. Pipe
around edge and decorate with the caramel triangles.

INGREDIENTS

Cuts into 10-12 slices

4 eggs

½ cup sugar

¾ cup self-rising flour

⅓ cup unsweetened cocoa
powder

¼ cup butter, melted and
cooled

¾ cup + 2 tbsp sugar

¾ cup prepared chocolate
buttercream (see page 8)

¾ cup shelled
pistachio nuts, chopped

Chocolate Fudge Cake

INGREDIENTS

Cuts into 12 slices

¾ cup butter
¾ cup light brown sugar
6 eggs, separated
4 oz semisweet chocolate,
melted
1 tbsp brandy
½ cup blanched almonds,
very finely ground
1 cup self-rising flour
1 tbsp unsweetened cocoa
powder, sifted

For the icing
2 cups confectioners'
sugar
2 tbsp unsweetened cocoa
powder
6 tbsp shortening
3 tbsp light cream
⅓ cup light brown sugar

gold and silver edible
balls to decorate

1   Preheat oven to 350°F. Lightly oil and line the bottom of an 8½-inch spring-form pan that is 3 inches deep.

2   Cream the butter and sugar together in a bowl until light and fluffy. Add the egg yolks one at a time, beating well.

3   Fold in the chocolate and the brandy, then mix lightly. Stir in the ground almonds, flour, and cocoa powder.

4   Beat the egg whites until stiff, then fold them into the batter. Spoon the batter into the prepared pan and bake for 45 to 55 minutes until a toothpick inserted in the center comes out clean. Remove from the oven and cool on a cooling rack before cutting in half crosswise.

5   To make the icing, sift the confectioners' sugar and cocoa powder into a bowl. Heat the shortening, cream and sugar, stirring, until the sugar dissolves, then bring to a boil. Pour onto the confectioners' sugar, and cocoa powder, then beat until thick and fluffy.

6   Spread the 2 halves with a little of the icing and sandwich together. Cover the cake with the remaining icing, swirling with a spatula. Decorate with gold or silver edible balls.

Truffle Gateau

1   Preheat oven to 400°F. Lightly oil and line a 13 x 9 x 2-inch jelly-roll pan.

2   Place the eggs and sugar in a large bowl over a pan of simmering water, then beat until thick and creamy. Remove from the heat and stir in the brandy or fruit juice, then fold in flour, cocoa powder, and ground almonds.

4   Spoon the batter into the prepared pan and bake for 12 to 15 minutes until firm to the touch. Cool before turning out, discarding the lining paper, and cutting crosswise into 3 equal pieces.

5   To make the filling, place the chocolate, cream and brandy in a heavy-bottomed pan and heat, stirring occasionally, until the chocolate melts and is smooth.

6   Remove from the heat, pour into a bowl and chill until cool. Beat until the mixture becomes thick and fluffy.

7   Spread one piece of cake with about 2 tbsp of the prepared filling, then place another piece of cake on top. Repeat layers, finishing with a layer of cake.

8   Cover the top and sides completely with the remaining filling and mark with a fork. Decorate with chocolate shells.

INGREDIENTS

Cuts into 12 slices

3 eggs

⅓ cup sugar

1 tbsp brandy or fruit juice

¾ cup self-rising flour, sifted

1 tbsp unsweetened cocoa powder

½ cup blanched almonds, very finely ground

For the filling
12 oz semisweet chocolate

1½ cups heavy cream

3 tbsp brandy

white and semisweet chocolate shells

No-Bake Crumb Cake

INGREDIENTS

Cuts into 8 bars

½ cup butter or margarine

6 tbsp light brown sugar

2 tbsp milk

4 oz semisweet chocolate

½ cup finely chopped no-need-to-soak dried apricots

½ cup raisins

⅓ cup candied cherries, chopped

1½ cups Graham cracker crumbs

confectioners' sugar to dredge

1 Lightly oil a 7-inch square baking pan.

2 Place the butter or margarine, sugar, and milk in a heavy-bottomed pan.

3 Break the chocolate into small pieces and add to the pan.

4 Heat gently, stirring occasionally until the mixture melts and is smooth. (Do not allow to boil.)

5 Remove from the heat, then stir in the apricots, raisins, cherries, and cracker crumbs.

6 Pour the batter into the prepared tin and smooth the top. Leave to set in the refrigerator.

7 To serve, cut into portions and dust with confectioners' sugar.

COOK'S TIP
Store, covered, in the refrigerator. Vary the candied and dried fruits used.

White Chocolate Cake

1   Preheat oven to 350°F. Lightly dust a 10-inch tube pan with flour.

2   Sift the flour and half the sugar together 6 times.

3   In another bowl, beat the egg whites until softly peaking, then beat in the cream of tartar and salt.

4   Gradually beat in the remaining sugar, beating well.

5   Fold in the flour in 3 stages. Fold in the grated chocolate.

6   Spoon the batter into the prepared pan, bake for 30 to 40 minutes until firm and the top springs back when lightly touched.

7   Remove the cake from the oven and leave to cool upside down on a wire rack. When cool, remove the pan.

8   Place the sugar, egg whites, cream of tartar, and 4 tbsp water in a large bowl over a pan of gently simmering water. Beat until the mixture is softly peaking and holding its shape.

9   Frost the cooled cake, then decorate with a few rose petals.

INGREDIENTS

Cuts into 12 slices

¾ cup all-purpose flour

¾ cup + 2 tbsp sugar

5 egg whites

1 tsp cream of tartar

pinch of salt

2 oz white chocolate, grated

For the frosting
1¾ cups sugar

2 egg whites

pinch cream of tartar

rose petals to decorate

Chocolate Kugelhupf

INGREDIENTS

Cuts into 8 slices

3 eggs

¾ cup sugar

4 oz semisweet chocolate, melted

1¾ cups self-rising flour

1 tsp apple pie spice

1 cup slivered almonds

⅔ cup chopped mixed peel

⅔ cup chopped no-need-to-soak dried apricots

2 tbsp brandy

1 tbsp confectioners' sugar, sifted

few slivered almonds

1   Preheat oven to 300°F. Lightly oil and flour a kugelhupf pan or a deep 7-inch round cake pan.

2   Beat the eggs and sugar together until thick and creamy.

3   Beat in the chocolate until smooth.

4   Sift the flour and apple pie spice together, then gradually beat it into the chocolate mixture.

5   Add the nuts, peel, chopped dried apricots, and brandy and stir together lightly until blended.

6   Spoon the batter into the prepared pan, then bake for 1 hour, or until a toothpick inserted in the center comes out clean.

7   Remove from oven and leave to cool for 10 minutes, then invert onto a wire rack and leave until completely cool.

8   To serve, sprinkle with the confectioners' sugar and scatter with slivered almonds.

COOK'S TIP
Ensure you oil and flour the kugelhupf pan in all the grooves. Then, when the kugelhupf is cool, the pan can be easily removed.

Chocolate Madeira Cake

1   Preheat oven to 350°F. Lightly oil and line the bottom of a deep 7-inch cake pan.

2   Cream the butter or margarine and sugar together until light and fluffy, then gradually beat in the eggs with a little sifted flour.

3   Fold in the remaining flour.

4   Sift the baking powder and sweetened cocoa powder and fold into the mixture.

5   Spoon the batter into the prepared pan and smooth the top.

6   Bake for 1 hour, or until a toothpick inserted into the center comes out clean. Remove from the oven and leave to cool on a wire rack before removing from the pan and discarding the lining paper.

7   To make the icing, sift the confectioners' sugar and cocoa powder into a bowl, then add the butter.

8   Stir in 1-1½ tbsp of boiling water and mix to make a smooth, spreadable icing.

9   Spread the icing over the top and sides of the cake, swirling with a spatula to give a decorative finish.

INGREDIENTS

Cuts into 12 slices

½ cup butter or margarine

½ cup sugar

3 eggs, beaten

¾ cup self-rising flour

1 level tsp baking powder

1 cup sweetened cocoa powder

For the icing
1½ cups confectioners' sugar

1 tbsp unsweetened cocoa powder

2 tbsp butter or margarine

Chocolate Jelly Roll

INGREDIENTS

Cuts into 10 slices

3 eggs

6 tbsp sugar

¾ cup self-rising flour

1 tbsp unsweetened cocoa
powder, sifted

1 tbsp sugar

For the filling
½ cup prepared vanilla
buttercream (see page 8)

½ cup chocolate pieces

confectioners' sugar to
dredge and chocolate
leaves to decorate

1   Preheat oven to 400°F. Lightly oil and line the bottom and sides of a jelly-roll pan with a sheet of parchment paper or foil.

2   Place eggs and sugar in a large bowl over a pan of gently simmering water, then beat until thick. Remove the bowl from the pan and beat until cool. Sift the flour and cocoa powder together, then gently fold into the beaten mixture.

3   Pour the batter into the prepared pan and tap the pan lightly on a surface to level the top. Bake for 12 to 15 minutes until the top is springy to the touch.

4   Have ready a large sheet of waxed paper, sprinkled with the sugar. Invert the cake onto the waxed paper and discard the lining paper. Roll up, encasing the waxed paper. Leave to cool.

5   Reserve 1 tbsp of the buttercream, then place the remainder in a small bowl and fold in the chocolate pieces. Unroll the jelly roll, remove the paper and spread with the buttercream.

6   Roll up again and dredge top with the confectioners' sugar, pipe small rosettes of buttercream on top and decorate with chocolate leaves.

Chocolate Fruit Cake

1   Preheat oven to 350°F.
Lightly oil and line the bottom of
a deep 7-inch cake pan with nonstick baking parchment.

2   Cream the butter and sugar together until light and fluffy.

3   Gradually add the beaten eggs to the creamed mixture, adding a little flour each time.

4   Stir in the melted chocolate, then the remaining flour with 1 to 2 tbsp of cooled, boiled water. Mix to make a soft dropping consistency. Stir in the dried and candied fruits.

5   Spoon the batter into the cake pan and sprinkle with the slivered almonds and sugar.

6   Bake for 1 to 1¼ hours until a toothpick inserted into the center comes out clean.

7   Leave to cool in the pan on a wire rack before turning out and discarding the lining paper.

COOK'S TIP
To test for dropping consistency, place a small amount of batter onto a spoon, then gently shake it back into the bowl. If it falls off easily, but does not run off, the consistency is correct.

INGREDIENTS

Cuts into 10-12 slices

½ cup butter

6 tbsp sugar

3 eggs, beaten

2 cups self-rising flour

3 oz semisweet chocolate, melted

1 cup golden raisins

½ cup cut mixed candied peel

⅓ cup chopped candied pineapple

1 tbsp slivered almonds

1 tbsp sugar

Chocolate-Date Quick Bread

INGREDIENTS

Cuts into 10-12 slices

½ cup butter or margarine

2¼ cups self-rising flour

½ cup light brown sugar

1 cup finely chopped
pitted dates

2 ripe bananas, mashed

2 eggs, beaten

3 oz semisweet chocolate,
melted

2 to 3 tbsp milk

butter or low-fat spread
for serving

1   Preheat oven to 350°F. Lightly oil and line the bottom of a 9 x 5-inch loaf pan.

2   Cut the butter or margarine into the flour until the mixture resembles fine bread crumbs.

3   Stir in the sugar, dates, and bananas.

4   Stir in the eggs with the melted chocolate.

5   Mix lightly, adding enough milk to make a soft dropping consistency. Spoon the batter into the prepared pan and smooth the top.

6   Bake for 1 hour, or until a toothpick inserted in the center comes out clean. Remove from oven and cool before removing from the pan and discarding the lining paper.

7   Store in an airtight container. Serve with a little butter or low-fat spread.

Chocolate and Cherry Cake

1   Preheat oven to 350°F. Lightly oil and line the bottom of a deep 7-inch round cake pan.

2   Cut the butter or margarine into the flour until the mixture resembles fine bread crumbs. Stir in the sugar, ground almonds, and shredded coconut.

3   In another bowl, beat the eggs with the almond extract, then add to the mixture and stir in lightly. Stir the chocolate to ensure it is smooth, then beat it into the batter.

4   Wash and dry the cherries thoroughly, then cut them in half. Fold them into the batter.

5   Spoon the batter into the prepared pan and smooth the top. Bake for 45 to 50 minutes until a toothpick inserted into the center comes out clean.

6   Leave to cool in the pan on a cooling rack before turning out and discarding the lining paper.

COOK'S TIP
When adding candied cherries to the batter, fold them in quickly and do not overmix or they may sink to the bottom.

INGREDIENTS

Cuts into 10 slices

¾ cup butter or margarine

1½ cups self-rising flour

¾ cup + 2 tbsp sugar

½ cup blanched almonds, very finely ground

⅔ cup shredded coconut

3 eggs

½ tsp almond extract

3 oz semisweet chocolate, melted

⅔ cup candied cherries

Chocolate Panettone

INGREDIENTS

Cuts into 12 slices

3 ½ cups all-purpose flour

4 tsp active-dry yeast

1 tsp light brown sugar

¾ cup warm milk

1 egg

2 egg yolks

½ cup butter, melted

4 oz semisweet chocolate, grated

grated zest of 1 orange

butter or low-fat spread to serve

1   Lightly oil and line the bottom and side of a deep 6-inch cake pan. Tie a collar of paper around the pan to stand 3 inches above the top.

2   Sift flour into a bowl, then stir in the yeast and sugar.

3   Beat the warm milk with the egg and egg yolks, then gradually add it to the flour and beat well to make a dough. (Add a little extra milk if necessary.) Beat in the melted butter, then leave to cool. Stir in the chocolate and orange zest. Knead on a lightly floured surface until pliable.

4   Place in a lightly oiled bowl, cover, and leave in a warm place to rise for about 1 hour, or until doubled in size.

5   Preheat oven to 400°F. Knead the dough again until smooth, then form into a smooth ball and place in the cake pan. Cover and leave until the dough rises to the top of the collar.

6   Mark a cross in the center of the risen dough. Bake for 10 minutes, then reduce oven temperature to 350°F and continue baking for 30 to 40 minutes until baked through.

7   Leave to cool in the pan, then discard lining paper. Serve cut in slices and spread with a little butter or low-fat spread.

Chocolate-Cinnamon Ring

1   Preheat oven to 375°F. Lightly oil a 10-inch tube pan and dust with flour.

2   Cream the butter or margarine and sugar together until light and fluffy. Beat in the egg yolks, one at a time, beating well.

3   Stir in the ground almonds, cinnamon, and grated chocolate. Sift the flour and baking powder together, then stir into the creamed mixture.

4   Beat the egg whites until they stand in peaks, then fold into the batter a little at a time. Spoon the batter into the prepared pan and smooth the top. Bake for 35 to 45 minutes until the top springs back when lightly touched.

5   Turn off the oven, leave the door open and let the cake cool in the oven for 20 minutes. Turn out of the pan and leave to cool on a wire rack.

6   Sift the confectioners' sugar and mix with 1-1½ tbsp very hot water. Stir until smooth and of a coating consistency. Drizzle the icing over the top of the cake, then sprinkle with a little flaked or grated chocolate.

COOK'S TIP
For an Easter treat, fill the hollow with mini chocolate eggs.

INGREDIENTS

Cuts into 12 slices

½ cup butter or margarine

½ cup sugar

3 eggs, separated

½ cup blanched almonds, very finely ground

1 tsp ground cinnamon

2 oz semisweet chocolate, grated

1 cup self-rising flour

½ tsp baking powder

4 tbsp confectioners' sugar, sifted

flaked chocolate

Chocolate Meringues

INGREDIENTS

Makes 12

2 egg whites

½ cup sugar

1 oz semisweet chocolate, grated

⅔ cup whipping cream

1 tbsp Crème de Caçao (optional)

chocolate triangles to decorate

1   Preheat oven to 250°F. Line a baking sheet with nonstick baking parchment.

2   In a bowl, beat the egg whites until stiff and dry. Gradually beat in half the sugar, 1 tbsp at a time, bringing the egg whites back to their original stiffness after each addition.

3   When half the sugar is added, fold in the remaining sugar and then the grated chocolate, mixing together lightly.

4   Pipe or spoon 24 small meringues onto the lined baking sheet. Place in the oven to dry out (about 2 hours, although this will depend on the size of the meringues).

5   Whip the cream until thick, then fold in the Crème de Caçao. Use to sandwich the meringues together. Place in paper bake cups and decorate with small triangles of chocolate.

COOK'S TIP
Ensure that your bowl and beaters are completely free from grease, otherwise the egg whites will not whisk satisfactorily and the meringues will not hold their shape. Use a rubber spatula in a figure-of-eight movement to fold in the sugar and grated chocolate. Take care not to overmix.

Maori Kisses

1 Preheat oven to 375°F. Lightly oil 2 baking sheets.

2 Cream the butter and sugar together until soft and fluffy, then stir in the flour and cocoa powder.

3 Stir in the chopped dates and walnuts, then mix with enough milk to bind the ingredients together to make a stiff mixture.

4 Place 8 small teaspoonfuls on the baking sheets, leaving a space in between to allow for spreading during baking.

5 Bake for 15 to 20 minutes until set. Remove from the oven and leave to cool for 2 minutes before transferring to a wire cooling rack. Leave to cool, then sandwich together with vanilla buttercream.

VARIATION
Sandwich 2 Maori Kisses together with whipped cream. Eat the same day.

INGREDIENTS

Makes 8

6 tbsp butter

6 tbsp light brown sugar

1 cup self-rising flour, sifted

1 tbsp unsweetened cocoa powder, sifted

1 cup chopped pitted dates

½ cup chopped walnuts

1 to 1½ tbsp milk

½ cup vanilla buttercream (see page 8)

Harlequin Towers

INGREDIENTS

Makes 8

½ cup butter

½ cup sugar

2 eggs

¾ cup self-rising flour, sifted

2 tbsp blanched almonds, very finely ground

1 tsp vanilla extract

1 tbsp unsweetened cocoa powder, sifted

3 tbsp apricot glaze (see page 8)
1 cup shredded coconut

1 tbsp buttercream (see page 8)
chocolate buttons

1   Preheat oven to 350°F. Lightly oil 8 dariole molds.

2   Cream the butter and sugar together until light and fluffy. Beat the eggs and add to the mixture a little at a time, with 1 tbsp of flour after each addition.

3   Stir in the remaining flour with the ground almonds and vanilla extract. Mix to a smooth dropping consistency with 1 tbsp cooled, boiled water.

4   Divide the batter into 2 portions and stir the cocoa powder into one portion. Place alternate spoonfuls in the molds to within ½ inch of their tops. Smooth the surfaces.

5   Place on a baking sheet and bake for 20 minutes or until slightly coming away from the sides of the molds.

6   Remove from oven and leave to cool before turning out and leaving until completely cool. Trim the bottoms if necessary so the towers stand upright.

7   Brush the baked towers with the apricot glaze, then roll in the shredded coconut until completely coated. Decorate each with a small rosette of buttercream and a chocolate button.

Chocolate-Coconut Chews

1   Preheat oven to 350°F. Lightly oil a 7-inch square baking pan.

2   Cream the butter, sugar, and cocoa powder together.

3   Stir in the flour, shredded coconut and milk, then knead lightly until the dough comes together.

4   Turn the dough into the pan, pressing it well down. Smooth the top with a spatula.

5   Bake for 20 to 25 minutes until firm to the touch and golden on top. Remove from the oven and cool on a wire cooling rack.

6   To make the icing, mix the confectioners' sugar with 1 to 1½ tbsp boiled water to make a smooth coating consistency.

7   Pour over the baked base, then pipe thin lines of melted chocolate across the top. Drag a thin skewer in the opposite direction to feather the icing, and, when cool, mark into 9 squares.

INGREDIENTS

Makes 9 squares

½ cup butter, softened

¼ cup dark brown sugar

1 tbsp unsweetened cocoa powder, sifted

1 cup all-purpose flour, sifted

2 cups shredded coconut

2 tbsp milk

For the icing
1½ cups confectioners' sugar, sifted

½ oz semisweet chocolate, melted

Chocolate Muffins

INGREDIENTS

Makes 9

1½ cups all-purpose flour

½ cup self-rising whole wheat flour

1 level tsp baking powder

¼ cup light brown sugar

1 cup blueberries

3 oz semisweet chocolate

¾ cup butter or margarine

2 eggs, beaten

3 tbsp buttermilk or plain yogurt

1   Preheat oven to 400°F. Line 9 muffin molds with paper bake cups.

2   Sift the flours and baking powder into a bowl, then stir in the sugar and blueberries.

3   Melt the chocolate and butter or margarine together in a pan over low heat. Leave to cool slightly, then beat in the eggs and buttermilk or yogurt. Beat until thoroughly blended.

4   Stir the chocolate mixture into the flours and mix well to make a stiff batter.

5   Spoon the batter into the bake cups, filling each one two-thirds full. Bake for 15 minutes, or until well risen and a toothpick inserted in the center of each comes out clean. Remove from the oven and, if possible, serve warm.

VARIATION
Substitute dried fruits or chopped nuts for the blueberries.

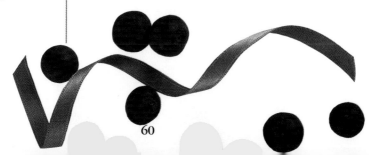

Truffle Cakes

1   Crumble the cake finely into a bowl.

2   Add the raisins, apricots and cherries, then mix well.

3   Break the chocolate into small squares, then place in a small, heavy-bottomed pan with the jam. Heat gently, stirring occasionally, until the mixture melts and is smooth.

4   Pour the melted chocolate mixture over the cake crumbs and fruit, then mix together well.

5   When cool enough to handle, shape into small balls about the size of a tangerine.

6   Place the chocolate jimmies on a piece of waxed paper and roll the balls in the jimmies until they are thoroughly coated.

7   Place in paper bake cups to serve.

VARIATION
Use shredded coconut as an alternative coating and try adding 2 tbsp rum or fruit juice to the mixture with ¼ cup extra crumbs.

INGREDIENTS

Makes 9

3 cups stale cake cubes

⅓ cup raisins

½ cup finely chopped no-need-to-soak dried apricots

⅓ cup chopped candied cherries

4 oz semisweet chocolate

2 tbsp apricot jam

1 cup chocolate jimmies

Chocolate Flapjacks

INGREDIENTS

Serves 8

½ cup butter or margarine

2 tbsp light brown sugar

3 oz semisweet chocolate, melted

2 tbsp light corn syrup

2½ cups quick-cooking oatmeal

½ cup pine kernels

½ oz semisweet chocolate, grated

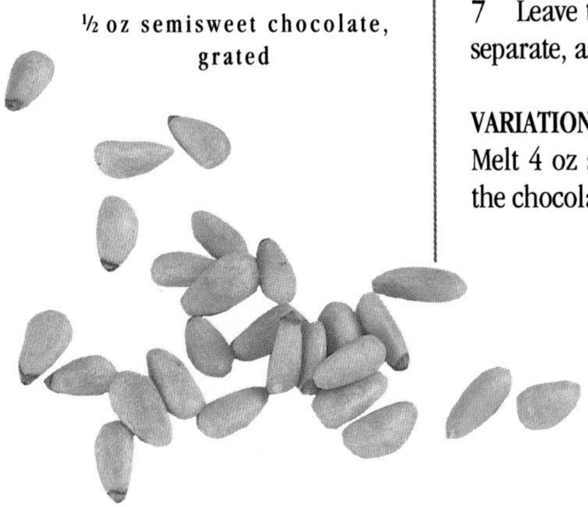

1   Preheat oven to 375°F. Lightly oil a 7-inch square baking pan.

2   Cream the butter or margarine with the sugar until light and fluffy.

3   Melt the chocolate and corn syrup together, stirring until smooth, then add to the creamed mixture and mix together well.

4   Stir in the oatmeal and pine kernels and mix together, then press into the prepared pan.

5   Bake for 20 minutes, or until firm to the touch.

6   Remove from the oven and mark into portions.

7   Leave to cool in the pan on a wire cooling rack, then remove, separate, and sprinkle with grated chocolate.

VARIATION
Melt 4 oz semisweet chocolate and use it to cover the top. Leave the chocolate to set before cutting the flapjacks into portions.

Chocolate Butterfly Cupcakes

1   Preheat oven to 375°F. Line 12 muffin molds with paper bake cups.

2   Cream together the butter and sugar until light and fluffy.

3   Beat in the eggs, a little at a time, with 1 tbsp of the flour after each addition.

4   Stir in the melted chocolate, then the remaining flour with 1-2 tbsp cooled, boiled water to make a soft dropping consistency.

5   Spoon the batter into the paper bake cups, then bake for 15 minutes, or until cooked and firm to the touch. Remove from the oven and leave until cold on a wire rack.

6   Cut out a small circle from the center of each cooked cupcake. Cut each circle in half.

7   Place the prepared buttercream in a decorating bag fitted with a star tip, then use to fill the hollows in each cake.

8   Place the 2 cut halves on top to represent butterfly wings and sprinkle with a little sifted confectioners' sugar and cocoa powder.

INGREDIENTS

Makes 12

½ cup butter

½ cup sugar

2 eggs, beaten

1 cup self-rising flour, sifted

2 oz semisweet chocolate, melted

½ cup prepared vanilla buttercream (see page 8)

2 tsp confectioners' sugar, sifted

2 tsp unsweetened cocoa powder, sifted

Fudge Brownies

INGREDIENTS

Makes 15

½ cup butter

4 oz semisweet chocolate

½ cup sugar

¾ cup dark brown sugar

2 eggs, beaten

¾ cup all-purpose flour

pinch of salt

½ tsp baking soda

1 tsp vanilla extract

¾ cup pecan nuts, chopped

1 oz white chocolate, melted

1   Preheat oven to 350°F. Lightly oil a 10 x 7-inch baking pan.

2   Melt the butter and chocolate in a heavy-bottomed pan over low heat. Stir until smooth. Add the sugars and continue to heat gently, stirring occasionally until the sugars dissolve. Remove from the heat.

3   Leave the mixture to cool slightly, then beat in the eggs gradually, beating well until the mixture is smooth and glossy. Stir in the remaining ingredients, except the melted white chocolate, and mix together well.

4   Spoon the batter into the prepared pan and bake for 25 to 30 minutes until a toothpick inserted into the center comes out clean. Take out of the oven and mark into 15 squares. Leave until cool before removing from the pan.

5   Place the melted white chocolate in a decorating bag fitted with a fine round tip, then pipe thin lines across each square.

VARIATIONS
Substitute walnuts or chopped blanched almonds for the pecan nuts. Another option is to add raisins or chopped candied fruits to the basic batter.

Chocolate Cups

1   Break the chocolate into small pieces and place it in a bowl over a pan of gently simmering water. Heat until the chocolate melts, then remove from heat and stir until smooth.

2   Using a pastry brush, brush the insides of 6 paper bake cups and leave the chocolate to set. Repeat, then leave in a cool place until firm. Peel away the paper cups, leaving the chocolate cups.

3   Cut the pound cake slices into small cubes and arrange in the bottom of the chocolate cups. Sprinkle with the Cointreau.

4   Cream the mascarpone cheese, sugar, and orange zest together until light and creamy.

5   Cut the orange segments into small pieces, then fold them into the cheese mixture.

6   Place on top of the pound cake cubes and smooth the surface.

7   Whip the cream until thick, then put it in a decorating bag fitted with a star tip and pipe a large rosette on top of each cake.

8   Dust with a little cocoa powder and serve decorated with thin slices of kumquat and lemon balm.

INGREDIENTS

Makes 6

8 oz semisweet chocolate

3 slices pound cake

2 tbsp Cointreau

1 cup mascarpone cheese

1 tbsp sugar

1 tbsp grated orange zest

2 oranges, peeled and segmented

$\frac{2}{3}$ cup whipping cream

1 tsp unsweetened cocoa powder, sifted

6 kumquats

lemon balm

Chocolate Macaroons

INGREDIENTS

Makes 10

2 egg whites

6 tbsp sugar

½ cup blanched almonds,
very finely ground

2 oz semisweet chocolate,
grated

10 whole blanched
almonds

1   Preheat oven to 350°F. Line 2 baking sheets with rice paper or nonstick baking parchment.

2   Beat the egg whites until stiff and standing in peaks.

3   Fold in the sugar 1 tbsp at a time, beating well and bringing the egg whites back to their original stiffness.

4   Using a large metal spoon or rubber spatula, fold in the ground almonds and chocolate.

5   Pipe or place 10 spoonfuls of the dough onto the baking sheets, allowing room for spreading during baking.

6   Place a whole almond in the center of each, then bake for 15 to 20 minutes until firm to the touch. Remove from the oven and leave to cool slightly before transferring to a wire cooling rack to cool completely.

VARIATION
As an alternative, pipe or place tiny teaspoonfuls of the dough onto baking sheets, then bake for 8 to 10 minutes until firm. Leave until cold, then sandwich together with whipped cream.

Chocolate and Almond Crisps

1   Preheat oven to 350°F. Line 2 baking sheets with non-stick baking parchment.

2   Heat the butter, sugar, and corn syrup in a pan over low heat, stirring until the butter melts.

3   Remove from the heat and add the flour, cocoa powder, and almonds, then mix together lightly.

4   Place 20 small teaspoonfuls on the lined baking sheets, allowing room for spreading during baking.

5   Bake for 8 to 10 minutes until set.

6   Remove from the oven and leave to stand for 2 minutes on the baking sheets before transferring to a wire cooling rack.

7   Leave until completely cool before serving.

COOK'S TIP
To fill the crisps, mold round the bottoms of small egg cups and leave until cool. Fill with whipped cream and fresh fruit. Eat within 4 hours of filling.

INGREDIENTS

Makes 20

2 tbsp butter

2 tbsp light brown sugar

1 tbsp light corn syrup

¼ cup all-purpose flour, sifted

1 tbsp unsweetened cocoa powder, sifted

⅓ cup slivered almonds

Chocolate Chip Cookies

INGREDIENTS

Makes 10

½ cup butter or margarine, softened

6 tbsp light brown sugar

1 egg, beaten

1½ cups all-purpose flour

⅓ cup semisweet chocolate pieces

1 Preheat oven to 350°F. Lightly oil 2 baking sheets.

2 Cream the butter or margarine and sugar together until light and fluffy.

3 Beat in the egg with 2 tbsp of the flour, then mix together well until thoroughly blended.

4 Add the remaining flour and the chocolate pieces and, using your hands, work the dough until it forms a ball in the center of the bowl.

5 Wrap and chill the dough for at least 30 minutes.

6 Using your hands, roll the chilled dough into 10 small balls, each about the size of an apricot, then place them on the prepared baking sheets, leaving sufficient space in between to allow for spreading during baking.

7 Bake for 15 to 20 minutes until pale golden. Remove from the oven and leave to cool for 2 minutes before transferring to a wire cooling rack. Leave until cold.

COOK'S TIP
The dough can be wrapped and stored in the refrigerator for up to 1 week, then baked as required.

Chocolate Pinwheels

1   Preheat oven to 375°F.
Lightly oil 2 baking sheets.

2   Cream the butter or margarine and sugar until light and fluffy, then beat in the egg. Place half the mixture in another bowl. Stir the melted chocolate into one half and mix well.

3   Add half the flour to the chocolate mixture, then knead until it forms a soft dough. Repeat with the other half of the mixture, adding the vanilla extract and then the remaining flour. Wrap both mixtures in waxed paper and chill for at least 30 minutes.

4   On a lightly floured surface, roll out both doughs into 6 x 4-inch rectangles. Brush the vanilla-flavored dough with a little water and place the chocolate-flavored dough on top. Roll up together like a jelly roll.

5   Using a sharp knife, cut into 12 thin slices and place on the baking sheets. Chill for a further 30 minutes.

6   Bake for 10 to 15 minutes (depending on thickness) until set. Leave to cool for 2 minutes on baking sheets before transferring to a wire cooling rack. Leave until completely cool.

INGREDIENTS

Makes about 12

6 tbsp butter or margarine

6 tbsp sugar

1 egg, beaten

2 oz semisweet chocolate, melted

2 cups all-purpose flour

½ tsp vanilla extract

Chocolate Viennese Whirls

INGREDIENTS

Makes 20

½ cup margarine, softened

6 tbsp unsalted
butter, softened

¾ cup confectioners'
sugar, sifted

3 oz semisweet chocolate,
melted

1 tbsp cornstarch, sifted

1 cup self-rising flour

1 cup all-purpose flour

½ cup prepared vanilla
buttercream (see page 8)

1   Preheat oven to 350°F. Lightly oil 2 baking sheets.

2   Cream the margarine, butter, and sugar together until light and fluffy. Beat in the melted chocolate, then the cornstarch.

3   Gradually add the sifted flours, a little at a time, beating well until smooth and stiff enough for piping.

4   Place the mixture in a decorating bag fitted with a large star tip and pipe 40 small whirls onto the baking sheets.

5   Bake for 12 to 15 minutes until firm to the touch. Remove from the oven and leave to cool for 2 minutes before transferring to wire cooling racks.

6   Sandwich the whirls together with the prepared buttercream.

COOK'S TIP
It is important that the fats are at room temperature and the flours sifted. Don't put too much mixture in the decorating bag.

Florentines

1   Preheat oven to 350°F. Lightly oil 2 baking sheets.

2   Rinse and dry the cherries, angelica, and pineapple, then chop together finely.

3   Place the butter or margarine, sugar, and corn syrup in a heavy-bottomed pan and heat gently, stirring occasionally.

4   Remove from the heat, then add the cherries, angelica, pineapple, golden raisins, and flour and mix together.

5   Place 10 small spoonfuls onto the baking sheets, then bake for 8 to 10 minutes until golden in color.

6   Leave to cool for 1 to 2 minutes before transferring to a wire cooling rack to cool completely.

7   Stir chocolate until smooth. Remove florentines from baking sheets and coat the bottoms with the melted chocolate. Using a fork, make a swirl pattern. Leave until set before serving. Store in an airtight container.

VARIATION
Place coffeespoonfuls onto the baking sheets, cook for 4 to 6 minutes, coat as above, and serve as petits fours.

INGREDIENTS

Makes 10

½ cup candied cherries

1 oz angelica

¼ cup finely chopped candied pineapple

¼ cup butter or margarine

3 tbsp light brown sugar

1 tbsp light corn syrup

⅓ cup golden raisins

½ cup all-purpose flour, sifted

6 oz semisweet chocolate, melted

Chocolate Dodgers

INGREDIENTS

Makes 10

1 ¼ cups + 1 tbsp all-
purpose flour

1 tbsp unsweetened cocoa
powder

¼ cup sugar

½ cup butter or
margarine, softened

½ cup prepared vanilla
buttercream
(see page 8)

1 tbsp confectioners'
sugar, sifted

1 tbsp shelled
pistachio nuts,
finely chopped

1   Preheat oven to 350°F. Lightly oil 2 baking sheets.

2   Sift the flour and cocoa powder together into a mixing bowl, then stir in the sugar.

3   Add the butter or margarine, then cut into the flour until the mixture resembles fine bread crumbs. Knead until the dough forms a ball in the center of the bowl and is smooth and pliable.

4   On a lightly floured surface, roll out the dough to about ½-inch thick. Using a 3-inch plain cookie cutter, stamp out about 20 circles. Then, with a ½-inch plain round cutter, stamp out the centers of half the circles and use remainder to cut more circles.

5   Place on the baking sheets and prick them lightly with a fork.

6   Bake for 15 minutes or until firm and slightly crisp around the edges. Leave to cool for 2 minutes before transferring to a cooling rack. Leave until completely cool.

7   Spread one plain round cookie with a little of the prepared buttercream and top with a cookie with the center cut out. Repeat until all the cookies have been sandwiched. Sprinkle the cookies with a little confectioners' sugar and add a few chopped pistachio nuts in the centers.

Chocolate Walnut Drops

1   Lightly oil a baking sheet.

2   Place the walnuts, sugar, butter or margarine, corn syrup, and honey in a heavy-bottomed pan with 2 tbsp of water.

3   Heat gently, stirring occasionally, until the sugar melts.

4   Increase the heat and boil steadily for 5 to 8 minutes until the mixture becomes light caramel in color.

5   Remove from the heat and place the bottom of the pan in a bowl of cold water. (This will stop the mixture cooking any more.)

6   Place 12 spoonfuls onto the baking sheet and leave to set for 20 minutes.

7   Melt the chocolate and stir until smooth, then remove the Walnut Drops from the baking sheet and coat the bottoms with chocolate. Using a spoon, swirl the chocolate over the flat bottoms. Leave to set.

INGREDIENTS

Makes 12

1 cup walnut halves

½ cup sugar

2 tbsp butter or margarine

2 tbsp light corn syrup

1 tsp honey

4 oz semisweet chocolate

Chocolate Grog

INGREDIENTS

Serves 1

2 oz semisweet chocolate

1 to 2 tbsp dark rum

1 cinnamon stick, lightly crushed

⅔ cup freshly made black coffee

light brown sugar to taste

2 tbsp whipped cream

1   Grate the chocolate, reserving 1 teaspoonful, and place in a small pan with the rum and cinnamon stick.

2   Heat gently, stirring occasionally, until the chocolate melts.

3   Discard the cinnamon stick, then add the coffee and sugar to taste. Stir until the sugar dissolves.

4   Pour into a heatproof glass, top with the cream, and sprinkle with the reserved grated chocolate.

5   Serve hot.

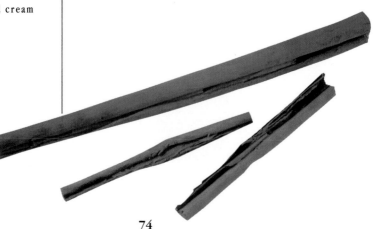

Chocolate Whip

1   Clean the fruit and rinse, then cut any large strawberries in half.

2   Place the fruit in a blender or food processor with the grated chocolate, honey, and milk.

3   Blend for 2 to 3 minutes, or until thoroughly mixed.

4   Pour into 4 tall glasses and add a scoop of yogurt to each.

5   Decorate with the fruit and serve immediately.

COOK'S TIP
You can vary the fruit and yogurt flavor according to preference. Try using vanilla ice cream for a change.

INGREDIENTS

Serves 4

½ lb fresh raspberries or strawberries

2 oz semisweet chocolate, grated

2 to 3 tbsp honey

3¾ cups chilled milk

4 scoops raspberry- or strawberry-flavored frozen yogurt

extra fruit to decorate

Iced Chocolate

INGREDIENTS

Serves 4

1 cup sugar

4 oz semisweet chocolate, grated

pared zest of 1 orange

3¾ cups milk, chilled

orange zest to decorate

1   Place the sugar with 1¼ cups water in a heavy-bottomed pan and heat gently, stirring, until the sugar dissolves.

2   Bring to a boil, then boil for 3 minutes, or until a light sugar syrup forms. Remove from the heat and stir in the chocolate and pared orange zest.

3   Stir until the chocolate melts, then cover and leave to cool, then chill.

4   When ready to serve, discard the orange zest from the chocolate syrup, then pour into a blender with the milk. (It's a good idea to do this in 2 batches.)

5   Blend for 2 minutes, then pour into tall glasses and add ice cubes. Decorate with a strip of orange zest secured with a toothpick. Serve immediately.

COOK'S TIPS

Prepare the chocolate syrup in advance and leave covered in the refrigerator. To make a delicious mocha-flavored drink, add 1 tbsp of instant coffee instead of the orange zest to the syrup.

Chocolate Truffles

1 Melt butter and chocolate in a heavy-bottomed pan, stirring frequently. Remove from heat and leave to cool, then beat in rum and egg yolks.

2 Gradually stir in the ground almonds, then ¾ cup of the confectioners' sugar, and beat until thoroughly mixed.

3 Place in a bowl, cover and chill in the refrigerator until set (about 1 hour).

4 Using your hands, roll the mixture into small balls. Roll the balls in the remaining confectioners' sugar, cocoa powder or chocolate jimmies, until completely coated. If liked, serve in petit four cases.

INGREDIENTS

Makes 12 oz

¼ cup butter

4 oz semisweet chocolate

1½ tbsp rum

3 egg yolks, beaten

½ cup blanched almonds, very finely ground

1 cup confectioners' sugar, sifted; ¼ cup unsweetened cocoa powder, sifted; or 4 oz chocolate jimmies

Chocolate and Raisin Fudge

INGREDIENTS

Makes 1¾ lb

3 oz semisweet chocolate

1¼ cups milk

1½ cups sugar

½ cup butter, diced

¾ cup raisins

1   Lightly oil a 7-inch square baking pan.

2   Break the chocolate into small pieces and place in a heavy-bottomed pan with the milk and sugar.

3   Place over low heat and cook, stirring throughout, until the sugar dissolves.

4   Add the butter and bring slowly to a boil, then boil steadily, stirring throughout, until the temperature is 240°F and the mixture forms a soft ball when a small amount is dropped into a bowl of cold water.

5   Remove from the heat and beat steadily with a wooden spoon until the mixture begins to thicken, then stir in the raisins.

6   Continue beating until the mixture is smooth, thick, and glossy. Pour into the prepared pan and mark into squares.

7   Leave until set before cutting through the squares and serving.

VARIATION
If liked, use chopped nuts instead of the raisins and add 2 tbsp rum to the mixture when adding the butter.

Chocolate Peppermint Creams

1 Beat the egg white until softly peaking, then beat in the cream of tartar and peppermint extract.

2 Add the confectioners' sugar a little at a time. As the mixture becomes stiff and hard to work, add 1 teaspoonful of the cream.

3 Add the green food coloring, if using, then turn out onto a surface lightly dusted with sifted confectioners' sugar. Knead the dough until smooth and pliable. Roll out to ½ inch thick.

4 Use a small cutter to cut out shapes. Place them on nonstick baking parchment or waxed paper and leave overnight.

5 Stir the melted chocolate until smooth, then half dip the creams into the chocolate, leaving them over the bowl for a few seconds to allow the excess chocolate to drip back. Place each on nonstick baking parchment or waxed paper until set. Alternatively, place the melted chocolate in a small decorating bag fitted with a plain round tip and pipe lines across the creams, then leave to set.

COOK'S TIPS
You can vary the flavor of the fondant cream by adding lemon, orange, coffee or rum extracts. For a special occasion, wrap the peppermint creams in colored cellophane paper.

INGREDIENTS

Makes 12oz

1 egg white

pinch cream of tartar

1 tsp peppermint extract

2 cups confectioners' sugar, sifted

3 tbsp whipping cream

a little natural green food coloring (optional)

4 oz semisweet chocolate

Index